"While being a pastor's wife is no [...] with hidden expectations and undefined [...] knowing intimately that the integrity of the man behind the pulpit holds enormous blessings, living in the constant, unyielding spotlight can weary the soul. A pastor's wife must learn how to feed on the word of God, turn the other cheek, cling to Christ, embrace the means of grace, protect her children from criticism and callings that they did not choose, and support a husband whose calling demands he lay down his life again and again. And all of this is done in the public eye. A pastor's wife needs a trustworthy friend, and she will find that friend in Jani Ortlund's book. Jani's wisdom has been refined by almost fifty years of being the wife of her pastor. Her writing style is simple, straightforward, and sane. Practical, poignant, and personal, this book is—like Jani—wise and tender and most of all, faithful to the call of Christ to join in the 'fellowship of His sufferings' (Phil. 3:10 NKJV). I love this book."

Rosaria Butterfield, Former Professor of English, Syracuse University; author, *The Gospel Comes with a House Key*

"Ministry wives today face both joys and challenges as they navigate their calling. Would that we could sit down with Jani Ortlund and learn from her wealth of wisdom from nearly fifty years of experience as an excellent wife alongside her pastor husband, Ray Ortlund. This book is the next best thing! Each short chapter tackles a timely challenge and then answers it biblically and specifically. Jani is one of the Lord's sweetest servants, and she embraces the high calling to be a pastor's wife to the glory of God. Jani loves Jesus and draws others to him. Jani loves Ray and inspires all of us who are ministry wives to serve more enthusiastically as we swim against the tide. Her writings are a gift. I am particularly eager to share this encouraging book with student wives as they prepare to serve our Lord and his church."

Mary K. Mohler, Director, Seminary Wives Institute, The Southern Baptist Theological Seminary; author, *Growing in Gratitude*

"I am thankful for this special and much-needed book—fresh, joyous, and written by someone who has been there and not found God to be wanting. What an encouragement to us ministry wives! It made me glad to be a pastor's wife, strengthened my hands for the work, and made me want to share this with my husband."

Carolyn Ash, wife of Christopher Ash, Writer-in-Residence, Tyndale House, Cambridge

"Oh, my goodness! I was hooked from the foreword to the very last prayer. I already knew I was going to love this book from my interaction with the gracious author, Jani Ortlund. However, I must say, this book exceeded my expectations! It is written with such warmth, humor, understanding, and grace. It is a must for every pastor's wife. Jani offers sage advice comingled with gentleness, understanding, affirmation, and oodles of encouragement. I plan on buying numerous copies of this book for women I know whose husbands are in God's service. Every chapter brought tears to my eyes, a smile to my face, and joy to my heart!"

Cheryl Brodersen, speaker; Bible teacher; Host, *Living Grace*; wife of Brian Brodersen, Pastor, Calvary Chapel Costa Mesa, California

"If you've lived as a ministry wife for more than ten seconds, you'll likely know how incredibly rewarding yet exceedingly difficult it can be. Jani Ortlund definitely does! This wonderful book is a treasure chest overflowing with refreshing, practical gems of wisdom, advice, and encouragement from a woman who has been there. Jani knows how to read the emotional dashboard of life as a ministry wife and then point us back to Jesus. Read this book slowly and soak up these truths; you'll find fuel for your journey and joy along the way."

Kristina Ramsey, pastor's wife and church planter, Liberti Church, Gold Coast, Australia

"The church is often aware of the chaos that comes with being a pastor, but the struggles of a pastor's wife are often overlooked. Jani Ortlund's motherly affection for younger pastors' wives shines through in *Help! I'm Married to My Pastor*. She disciples us at the turning of every page with her godly wisdom and love."

Nikki Daniel, wife of Bert Daniel, Pastor, Crawford Avenue Baptist Church, Augusta, Georgia

"Jani Ortlund invites pastors' wives and ministry leaders to drink from her deep well of biblical, practical wisdom. This book is a winsome reminder of why we must press on in our calling despite real hardships along the way. Jani is running with us, coaching us to press on toward the goal because Christ is worth it. Every married woman in ministry will be spurred to the finish line through her mentoring in *Help! I'm Married to My Pastor*. It's been added to my list of must-read books to equip and encourage women. I joyfully recommend it!"

Leslie Bennett, Director of Women's Ministry Initiatives, Revive Our Hearts

Help! I'm Married to My Pastor

*Encouragement for
Ministry Wives and Those
Who Love Them*

Jani Ortlund

WHEATON, ILLINOIS

Library of Congress Cataloging-in-Publication Data

Names: Ortlund, Jani, author.
Title: Help, i'm married to my pastor!: encouragement for ministry wives and those who love them / Jani Ortlund.
Description: Wheaton, Illinois : Crossway, 2021. | Includes bibliographical references and index.
Identifiers: LCCN 2020001987 (print) | LCCN 2020001988 (ebook) | ISBN 9781433569777 (trade paperback) | ISBN 9781433569784 (pdf) | ISBN 9781433569791 (mobi) | ISBN 9781433569807 (epub)
Subjects: LCSH: Spouses of clergy. | Wives–Religious life.
Classification: LCC BV4395 .O78 2021 (print) | LCC BV4395 (ebook) | DDC 253/.22–dc23
LC record available at https://lccn.loc.gov/2020001987
LC ebook record available at https://lccn.loc.gov/2020001988

Crossway is a publishing ministry of Good News Publishers.

BP		30	29	28	27	26	25	24	23	22	21
15	14	13	12	11	10	9	8	7	6	5	4	3	2	1

To Ray Ortlund Jr.
The truest and best of his generation
and the Christlike pastor I get to be married to.
I'm forever grateful.

Contents

Foreword

AN *UNSUNG HERO* IS defined as "one who does great deeds but receives little or no recognition for them." It's an accurate description of a pastor's wife, isn't it?

She pours out her life not only for her family but also, with her husband, for her church. She is not a life-depleting person but wonderfully life-enriching to all around. The world is more alive because she is alive. She is like Christ. Indeed, she is from Christ.

If you are the wife of a pastor, that's *you*. It's why you *so* matter. You are not always thanked as you deserve to be. So as you open this book, let me be the first to say *thank you!* Thank you for putting Christ first. Thank you for loving your pastor husband. Thank you for believing, for praying, for serving. We all owe you a great debt of gratitude.

This book matters because you matter. My amazing wife, Jani, wrote this for *you*—to affirm you and encourage you; to put some fresh wind into your sails; to help you feel noticed, understood, and respected; to invest in you and strengthen you and prepare you for your glorious future. She is glad this book is now in your hands. May the Lord himself add his blessing!

Let me tell you something about this book's author. Even as "there was a man sent from God, whose name was John" (John 1:6), there is also a woman sent from God, whose name is Jani. I have the sacred privilege of being her husband. Under Christ himself, she is God's greatest gift to me. She is a gift to you too, even as you are to so many.

I am glad Jani wrote this book. She is qualified to do so. She knows what she's writing about. When I was ordained to the gospel ministry in 1975, she was there, and she was all in. I can't remember a single Sunday in all these years when she wasn't there, praying for me and encouraging me, all in. Jani has seen it all and survived it all, and to this day she is still giving life—even more than ever.

I have never once seen Jani turn away and refuse the call of Christ upon her life. I have never once seen her return evil for evil. I have never once seen her sink into despair and rage. Time after time after time, she has put her trust in the Lord and bravely done the next right thing. And she has only grown deeper in Christ and richer in her capacity to give life. I owe her so much. The churches we have served owe her so much. My success is hers.

Now her hard-won experience over these many years is her gift to you—through this book. Maybe the best way to benefit from it is to read slowly, just one chapter at a time, sharing your thoughts with your husband along the way. At the end of each chapter, Jani includes a brief note to your husband as well, so that the two of you can experience the journey side by side. By the end, you'll be in a deeper place together, by God's grace, for his glory. And with you stronger, Jani will be happier too.

Thank you for giving Jani the privilege of serving you.

The LORD bless you and keep you;
The LORD make his face to shine upon you and be
    gracious to you;
The LORD lift up his countenance upon you and give you
    peace. (Numbers 6:24–26)

Ray Ortlund, Pastor to Pastors,
Immanuel Church, Nashville, Tennessee

Introduction

HER VOICE WAS UNKNOWN TO ME, but her story was all too familiar. "My husband is a pastor and I don't know who to talk to. Would you have time to meet?" Soon she was pouring out to me her heartache of discouragement, confusion, and broken relationships.

Ministry marriages bear unique strains that often obscure the joys of building a lifelong romance. A woman marries a man, not his ministry, but somehow her husband's calling seeps into every aspect of their one-flesh relationship. The weight of accurately teaching God's word week by week, the burden of bearing the confidential crises of his people, the responsibility of guiding friends through life's most significant events (births, baptisms, weddings, deaths), the obligation of leading a staff and lay leaders with competence, the task of raising up a godly family in a public setting, the call to live a life worthy of imitation in every way—these and other pastoral pressures can cause tension in any ministry marriage.

This book is for every ministry wife who has ever felt alone and fears she might not have what it takes to sustain a happy ministry marriage. It is, strangely enough, a validation of that fear. Who, after all, is truly capable of this calling?

This book is also an affirmation that God will work out his delightfully good purposes in and through her. Marriage to a pastor is a sacred calling. A ministry wife's fears about rumors and romance, finances and friendships, hospitality and home-making can all find a resting place in the one who called her into this ministry marriage. "He who calls you is faithful; he will surely do it" (1 Thessalonians 5:24).

What every ministry wife needs is a friend—not another list of things to do to keep everyone happy, but another woman calling back to her from farther down the road, telling her that this life of sacrifices is worth it because Jesus is worth it. I want to be that kind of friend, Lord willing, who will call back to those behind me, "Keep going! You may be in a muddle right now, but keep going! It will be worth it! We serve the God who remembers. He sees. He knows. He cares."

Help! I'm Married to My Pastor comes out of almost fifty years in a ministry marriage. Throughout our ministry I have experienced both successes and failures, shed tears of joy and tears of shame, spoken words of affirmation and words of gossip. I've loved Ray well, and I've hurt him deeply. But in it all, Jesus Christ has never forsaken me. He has guided and loved me and has given me a story to tell—a story filled with his mercy and strength in the midst of my own sin and weakness.

I want to share some of the ways our kind King has answered me when all I could cry out was, "Help! I'm married to my pastor!" I want to strengthen your soul in Christ and encourage you to continue in the faith (Acts 14:22).

I also want to help you build a bridge from your heart to that pastor you fell in love with. At the end of each chapter you'll find a letter I've written to your husband. See if he's interested in reading it and interacting with you. If not, lean on me and tell him with a twinkle in your eye, "Jani says that if you read her letters to you, I'm to make it worth your while!" Then, dear ministry wife, start thinking of a good prize for your pastor husband! Maybe you could read a book that *he* has suggested you read. Or maybe he has been wanting a guilt-free trip to the nearest sporting goods store for that new fishing pole or deer rifle (ask me how I know about this kind of treat). Or maybe he would enjoy a date night out that you arrange for the two of you. Or even a quiet evening at home alone with candles and a good movie and . . . The possibilities are endless. The idea is to show him your gratitude in a way that's meaningful to him. You'll both benefit, making it a real win-win blessing for your marriage.

Thank you for reading this book. Thank you for striving for the most satisfying and exemplary ministry marriage possible. As you read, I'm humbly praying that these words might sweeten and soften the sacrifices that every ministry wife makes. May God bless you more and more.

1

Help! I Didn't Bargain for This

WHATEVER YOUR STORY, we're in this crazy club together, this "I'm the preacher's wife" club that marks you in the eyes of anyone else who isn't. Some of you grew up hoping to marry a minister, and God gave you the desires of your heart. Others of you fell in love, and your man was heading toward the pastorate, so you followed him there. And some of you met, married, started work and your family, and then—wham! Your husband told you that God was calling him into ministry. You might still be trying to figure out what happened!

However you got here, you have joined that special group known as "ministry wives." Could I be your friend? Could we share a few hours together delighting in the joys and privileges of becoming one with a man set apart to lead the church of the living God? And may I bear with you some of the unique strains that flow from your calling in life as we look to the one who called us all?

They Act Like They Got Two for the Price of One

In our almost fifty years of ministry so far, I have never once met a wife who told me, "Jani, being a ministry wife is so much easier than I ever thought it would be! Every woman should be so fortunate as to have my role!" What I have heard, and sometimes felt myself, is:

> "Some people treat me as if pastoring is my job as well as my husband's."

> "I am not a pastorette! Why do people expect me to know all that is going on at church?"

> "I worked to put my husband through seminary. Why do some people expect me to be a biblical expert? I feel embarrassed and ignorant at times."

> "Women come to me for counsel, but I have had no real training. What if I make it worse?"

> "What if . . . ?" "Why . . . ?"

What I have heard is that the complexities of this role outweigh a wife's expectations and dreams. Most ministry wives want desperately to support and enhance their husband's service to Christ, but they feel like failures. They feel alone and fearful that they will never really measure up.

I want to tell you that you are *not* alone. You are not crazy. You didn't make a mistake in marrying that man. God knew exactly what he was doing when he brought the two of you together and kindled that extraordinary love in both of your hearts.

Long Ago

Think of all God has done to bring you to this very moment in your life. God, in eternity past, chose you to be an active soldier in his mighty rescue operation for this needy world.

The Bible says that long ago, before the very foundations of the world, God thought you up and chose you for his very own:

> . . . even as he chose us in him before the foundation of the world, that we should be holy and blameless before him. In love he predestined us for adoption to himself as sons through Jesus Christ, according to the purpose of his will. (Ephesians 1:4–5)

Long ago, before you were even born, God formed and numbered the days of your life:

> Your eyes saw my unformed substance;
> in your book were written, every one of them,
>> the days that were formed for me,
>> when as yet there was none of them. (Psalm 139:16)

Long ago God planned the path for your very own personal race in life—a race that only you can run:

> Therefore, since we are surrounded by so great a cloud of witnesses, let us also lay aside every weight, and sin which clings so closely, and let us run with endurance the race that is set before us. (Hebrews 12:1)

Long ago God decided and prepared good works that only you would walk in:

For we are his workmanship, created in Christ Jesus for good
works, which God prepared beforehand, that we should walk
in them. (Ephesians 2:10)

And then he stepped into time and made you in secret,
knitting you together in your mother's womb and brought you
forth into his world and revealed himself to you with irresistible
divine power and set you on your own personal pilgrimage to
spend eternity with him:

> For you formed my inward parts;
>   you knitted me together in my mother's womb. . . .
> My frame was not hidden from you,
> when I was being made in secret,
>   intricately woven in the depths of the earth.
>   (Psalm 139:13, 15)

Along the way, he introduced you to that godly man who
captured your heart. God caused a sweet fire to ignite between
you, and he brought you to your husband as his own personal
gift from the Lord:

> He who finds a wife finds a good thing
>   and obtains favor from the LORD. (Proverbs 18:22)

Let's learn to see the big picture of God's mighty purposes.
Our calling as women deeply involved in ministry is a vital part
of God's eternal plan. He knows, he sees, he cares. Your life as a
ministry wife may feel like so much more than you bargained
for. But God is in it, intimately involved and committed to helping you fulfill his call on your life (1 Thessalonians 5:24). Look
to him. Lean on him. It will be worth it.

——————— A LETTER TO YOUR PASTOR ———————

Dear Pastor,

Have you given your wife the freedom to open her heart to you? Why not ask her what is hard for her as a ministry wife? As she opens up, try not to correct her or defend yourself. Listen and empathize. Are there ways you can affirm her? By all means, do!

And why not ask your wife what expectations she feels from you and others? Decide together which ones to embrace as from the Lord and which ones can be safely disregarded (2 Corinthians 10:18). And then take her in your arms and pray for her and your ministry marriage. You'll be glad you did—and so will your flock!

Prayerfully,

Jani

2

Help! It's Sunday Morning

BEVERLY MARRIED A PASTOR, and their four children came in rapid succession. Sunday was the most stressful day of her week. Her husband left early to unlock the church and prepare for his morning of ministry. And getting her four little ones dressed, fed, and in their car seats single-handedly—never mind getting herself ready—proved overwhelming at times.

The Zoo Patrol

Knowing that she would need to cheerfully corral her little ones throughout the morning, while introducing herself to visitors and remembering the very real concerns of church members, added to her Sunday morning angst. By the time she pulled into the parking lot, she found her heart longing to escape to any other place on earth where there were fewer duties and expectations.

One Sunday as she was getting the kids out of the car, she couldn't find her two-year-old's diaper bag. She must have left it on the kitchen counter—again! When would he finally learn to use the potty? She could imagine his teacher's forced smile as she dropped him off empty-handed. And then she noticed something even more disheartening—she had on two different shoes! Looking back she would find it quite humorous, but not that Sunday.

What a blessing that Helen saw the tears brimming in Beverly's eyes as she walked by. After helping Beverly and the kids into church, Helen began thinking, and a few days later she told Beverly about a plan she and seven other ladies wanted to implement—a *zoo patrol*. Each Sunday morning, two of these understanding older women would arrive at Beverly's door one hour before church started to help her get her little zoo fed, dressed, and transported to church. What a happy bonus for everyone—pastor, pastor's wife, zoo patrollers, and four little ones who had someone to lovingly help them pour their milk and comb their hair and zip their jackets.

A Spoonful of Sugar

I never had a zoo patrol, but I often needed one! We lived in Scotland for four years while Ray earned his PhD from the University of Aberdeen. Ray assisted in our parish church and left early on Sunday mornings. It was hard for me to get our four kids ready and willing for our mile walk to church (we had no car at the time).

I had to do something to help with the complaints and tears and my own growing resentment. So I decided to try making Sunday morning our best morning of the week, something to anticipate rather than dread. I made sure on Saturday night that the children's clothes were ready without the needless friction of "I can't find my other shoe!" or "My zipper is broken." We often mixed up a fresh yeast dough on Saturday afternoon and had fun rolling out several cinnamon rolls to rise overnight. The children would wake up to that tantalizing aroma, which still brings us back in our hearts to our tiny kitchen there along Royal Deeside. Some scrambled eggs and fresh fruit rounded out our special Sunday breakfast.

After getting the dishes into the sink we would set out, and I had "sweeties" in my pocket to reward cheerful and quick obedience. We would have contests to see who could make it to the next driveway without complaining, or who could spot the next house with white flowers in the garden, or who could think of one thing they loved about their daddy before we reached the shop on the corner.

Along the way we would talk about what a special hour was before us, the one hour out of all 168 hours in each week where we could worship God together with our friends. I asked the older children to give me and others sitting near us the gift of sitting quietly for just this short time so we could pray and sing and listen. I encouraged them to try to join in as they were able. When I was first training them to sit quietly, I would sometimes reward them with more sweeties during the sermon.

Then on the way home, we would get the wiggles out with happy words about our time at church, and I'd offer many thanks for loving me, respecting the adults around us, and most of all honoring God with their quiet bodies and mouths. Around the lunch table I would brag to their daddy about their good behavior, and they would light up under his enthusiastic approval.

Was each Sunday as idyllic as I make it sound? No, indeed! There were Sundays when the cinnamon rolls burned, or one of us was in a foul mood, or—horror of horrors—I ran out of sweeties! Every Sunday I needed to rely on the Lord of the Sabbath for perseverance and patience, which he so kindly gave abundantly, overflowingly—"grace upon grace" (John 1:16).

But week by week it got a little easier as we started to embrace a pattern that brought us joy. Sunday morning became, with the Lord's help, a "We get to!" rather than a "Do we *have* to?" And, I might add, all four of our kids grew up with no cavities! I wonder if the Lord protected them from all my sugar bribes?

Instilling a Deep Love for Sunday Mornings

What I'm saying, dear ministry wife, is that you have the opportunity of passing on to your children a deep love for Sunday mornings. Children learn to love what their parents love. They will get excited about what excites you.

Let them see the sparkle in your eye when you tell them, "Guess what day it is tomorrow? Yes! It's Sunday!" Let them hear the genuine warmth in your voice when you say, "I can't wait to hear what Daddy will teach us all about God tomorrow." Let them feel the glorious privilege of corporate worship as you pray with them, "Thank you for our church and for this special day each week." Help them to "taste and see that the LORD is good!" (Psalm 34:8).

Yes, this will take extra work on your part. But it will be well worth it! Start small. Be creative. Ask the Lord to help you. Or pray for a "Helen" to help organize your own personal zoo patrol!

Your husband will thank you. Your church will benefit. Your own soul will be better able to feast on the abundance of his house (Psalm 36:8). And your kids will begin to say along with

King David, "I was glad when they said to me, 'Let us go to the house of the Lord!'" (Psalm 122:1).

──────────── A LETTER TO YOUR PASTOR ────────────

Dear Pastor,

What do you love about Sunday mornings? And what is hard for you about Sunday mornings? Could you share both with your wife and invite her response?

Then why not dream together about how you, as a team, can make Sunday mornings the best morning of the week for you and your family? How could you spend Saturday evening so that Sunday morning is less harried and hassled? What might you do to help your wife be at her best for worship? Maybe you could offer her time to get her hair and face done before she has full care of the children? What could she do to help you—cook you a healthy breakfast? Be honest and creative and joyfully united in your desire to instill in your children a deep love for Sunday morning and all it means.

You can give your children the strongest impression that worshiping Jesus at church is your deepest joy. Help your wife fill your children's little hearts with happy expectations for all that Sunday can bring to their lives.

Expectantly,

Jani

3

Help! I Want to Fix Him

AS A MINISTRY WIFE, you have the privilege of knowing intimately a man going hard after God and his word, a man who strives week after week, year after year, to communicate all that God gives him to the people God brings into his life.

Your Most Important Ministry in God's Kingdom Work

Now some would not think that knowing such a man intimately is such a great privilege. I once heard a ministry wife comment, "Clergy ought to be celibate because no decent right-minded man would have the effrontery to ask any woman to take on such a lousy job. It is thoroughly unchristian!"

It may be difficult, but it is not lousy.

It may be exhausting, but it is not indecent.

It may even be painful, but it is not unchristian.

Your marriage is God's gift to you. And it is a good and perfect gift. Your most important ministry in God's kingdom work is not to your church or even to your children. Your most important ministry is to your husband.[1] The best service you can offer to God's work in your generation is to be the most loving, fun, and supportive person your pastor will ever know.

Two Responses

We all want to be that kind of wife, but what about those vital areas where you think that your husband needs to adjust and change? What can you do when you want to help your husband by fixing him?

Following are two responses I've shown Ray, and I have found them most helpful when I've been tempted to fix him. You might want to try them too.

1. Show Him Appreciation and Loyalty

Extend grace to your pastor husband. He needs to be almost perfect for everyone else. Be a safe place for him to land.

When you live with constant pressure day after day, the tendency is to withdraw into your own protective castle surrounded by your personalized moat of defenses. It is my privilege as Ray's wife to be the one person to gain access to his castle by enticing him to let down his drawbridge. It's a learning process. Sometimes I storm in; sometimes I steal in. Whatever it takes in *your* marriage, learn the secret of getting in. And one clear pathway of access to his heart is to truly appreciate what he is trying to do with his life.

Your husband needs to know that you think he is really wonderful. Speak well of him to friends and family. Praise him in front of your kids. Is he late for dinner again? You have one of two ways to respond:

"*Poor me*—he's late again!" (as you bang the dishes onto the table).

Or

"*Poor Daddy*—let's pray for him. He must be so hungry and tired. Who can help me fix a plate for him to keep warm in the oven?"

Honor the work that he is doing by being flexible and respectful.

2. *Accept Him as He Is*

Men interpret advice as lack of approval. And your husband will get plenty of advice from others—his coworkers, his congregants, his family, even his Twitter followers! He needs to know you are on his side, that he's not standing alone. Let others try to improve him. In your eyes he needs to be okay. He is most likely all too aware of his own shortcomings anyway.

I am a fixer by nature. And besides that, people used to try to get to Ray through me, especially women. "I know how busy Ray is. Please tell him . . ." And they would go on with some complaint turned into a suggestion. Somehow I would try to let him know what they had told me, from which side of his suit coat he should put his name tag on, to how to pronounce a missionary's name, to who should be our next women's ministry leader. I tried to fix him according to their desires so that everyone would be happy. Hah! Now there's a demented fantasy.

I did try, that is, until one Sunday night after a very long week of intense ministry (and there I was fussing at him again over some insignificant recommendation from a congregant), he turned to me, took me in his arms, and fixed his big blue eyes on me, saying, "Darling, I need to know there is one person in this messy world who isn't trying to change me, who really likes me for who I am, even with my imperfections—someone willing to let the Holy Spirit be the main source of change in my life. Would you be willing to be that person for me?" You can imagine my response. Boy, was I! I certainly didn't want anyone else stepping up to apply for that position!

So I had to learn to say to others, "That's an interesting idea. Why don't you give the office a call and set up an appointment to discuss this with Ray? It would be much better coming directly from you than through me."

If there is something that you feel really needs changing, pray earnestly and often about it. Ask our wise Father to reveal it to your man through his Spirit or through another servant who works closely with him. And then you will have the glorious joy of seeing your pastor grow through the power of the Holy Spirit rather than the pain of a nagging wife.

Guard Your Spirit

Think of the blessings of marriage. You are chosen by someone, and you have the chance to choose someone for yourself. You enter into a relationship of trust and comfort and joy. You belong somewhere and with someone. You live out your own shared history. Marriage makes two people together what they could never be alone. Your shared love costs you more than you ever thought, but I promise it can give you more than you ever dreamed!

Yet in the midst of these blessings we face real disappointments:

- limited income

- a crazy schedule

- job insecurity

- spiritual malaise

- conflicts with the in-laws

- less than thrilling times of intimacy

- his inability to anticipate or even understand your needs

- the never-ending cares of his flock

How can you handle these disappointments? What is the antidote for the "fix-him fever" that attacks your spirit?

Begin by embracing the biblical reality that marriage is an unconditional commitment to an imperfect person. That commitment means a willingness to sometimes be unhappy. And in that unhappiness you must guard your spirit (Malachi 2:15). Unhappiness is not the worst experience in a marriage—unfaithfulness is.

The Ultimate Human Experience

I have been talking about making the most of your ministry marriage. But ultimately your marriage will be *only* as happy and satisfying and passionate as your relationship with Christ is.

In the hurts and disappointments of life, is Jesus enough, or are you looking to something else to save you from your loneliness or sadness or insecurity?

At times your love may be soured by the inevitable disappointments of living as one flesh with another human being. When that happens, look ahead to your heavenly husband, the lover of your soul, who loves you completely even as you are. He paid the greatest bride price imaginable to capture your heart and bring you into his loving embrace.

A woman is most beautiful when she knows she is loved. Your femininity is most radiant, nurturing, gracious, and other-centered when you know you are loved. Let God make you, through his tender and intimate love, the beautiful woman he created you to be.

And where do we find that love? Where do we warm our hearts with the love of God? At the foot of the cross. Never be content with your current grasp of the cross. Never feel that you have grown beyond your need for the cross. Keep close enough to the cross so that you can daily feel the warmth of God's redeeming love for you.

The most helpful way you can support and help, rather than trying to fix, the man God brought into your life is to find your soul's deepest fulfillment in Christ. If God's redeeming love is truly filling your heart, then God himself will be the ultimate human experience, not a perfect ministry or sterling reputation or sparkling marriage or you name it! "For God alone my soul waits in silence; from him comes my salvation" (Psalm 62:1). Why not come to God anew today? Ask him to restore your soul (Psalm 23:3) in fresh and intimate ways that will support a more deeply satisfying relationship with your heavenly husband.

——————— A LETTER TO YOUR PASTOR ———————

Dear Pastor,

Describe to your wife some of the current pressures you are under. She wants to be the most fun, loving, and supportive person in your life. But she may need some coaching. Use words like, "I feel supported when you . . ." or "I feel accepted by you when . . ."

Talk through strategies she could use when well-meaning people try to get to you through her. And then affirm her as she rises up from the "fix-him fever" to go hard after God together with you, more united than ever.

From a former fix-him-fever fanatic,

Jani

4

Help! My Husband
Seems Depressed

CHRISTIAN MINISTRY IS A crisis vocation because you are deal-ing with people, and people always have crises: death, illness, ac-cidents, divorce, rebellious kids, addictions, conflicts, deadlines.

A Crisis Vocation

Men in ministry are always under fire. A friend sent me a list of the characteristics of the perfect pastor. The list included these qualities:

- He preaches exactly twenty minutes and follows it with an invitation in which everyone is convicted but no one is offended.

- He is able to pastor at twenty-seven years old and has thirty years of preaching experience.

- He invests 25 hours a week on sermon prep, 20 hours in counseling, 10 hours in meetings, 5 hours dealing with emergencies, 20 hours doing visitation and evangelism, 6 hours at weddings and funerals, 30 hours in prayer and meditation, 12 hours on letter writing, 8 hours on administration, and 10 hours in creative thinking.

- He is a seminary graduate but uses only one- and two-syllable words.

- His kids are perfect.

- His mother is rich.

- His wife plays the piano.

- He is paid too much, and he gives most of it away.

- He is talented, gifted, scholarly, practical, popular, compassionate, understanding, patient, level-headed, dependable, loving, caring, neat, organized, cheerful, and, above all, humble.

The stress of ministry can become addictive because the adrenaline that stress produces is addictive. I wonder if your husband experiences a Monday morning post-adrenaline depression after giving so much all week? We don't have the time, and I don't have the training, to go deeply into this aspect of ministry, but let me say that whether for the sake of your own home and marriage or in order to help others, *learn how to deal with depression.*

Some statistics state that 10 percent of people gathered together anywhere are clinically depressed (i.e., needing treatment). Depression has been called the common cold of the emotions. But when we're depressed, we often feel guilty, and we won't acknowledge that we feel down. We are afraid to admit that we are struggling with the blues, fearing we will seem spiritually immature.

Strategic Dying

Depression is not a sin. It is oftentimes a healing emotion, helping us to cope with loss and stress and crises. Whether depression is biological or situational or psychological, do not use bad theology to try to deal with it. What kind of help will it be if you tell a depressed person that his depression is demonic?

Paul's theology of ministry is found in 2 Corinthians 4. We are all jars of clay (v. 7), and as such we are all very fragile. Verse 10 tells us that we are "always carrying in the body the death of Jesus." Ministry is all about dying—to our own rights, to our desires for prestige or financial gain, to our own self-protection—and learning to say with Paul, "For to me to live is Christ, and to die is gain" (Philippians 1:21).

But let's be wise in how we live out the deaths of gospel ministry. There is a difference between killing yourself and dying to yourself! "Let your ministry be strategic dying," I heard a psychologist say at a conference for ministers at Hilton Head, South Carolina, in 2000. He encouraged us to ask ourselves, "How can I accomplish the most by minimizing what's killing me and maximizing productivity for him?"

What is killing you these days? What is killing your husband? What drains you, sucking the life out of you? As best you can, choose which situations you will allow to become emergencies. Coach yourself to relax. Choose delays, slow routes, a longer checkout line at the market. Don't waste your adrenaline. You have a limited amount of emotional and psychological energy. Use it wisely.

A book I've found very helpful in this area is *Margin* by Richard Swenson.[2] Swenson teaches us how to come out from under the overload of fatigue and hurry and anxiety by enjoying the benefits of contentment, simplicity, balance, and rest. And if you're thinking you don't have time to read it, you're on overload. Please get it and read it! Then share it with your husband. It will help you both, as well as your church.

Recover through Rest and Relationships

Try to build in recovery after periods of high demands. Don't feel guilty when you take time off! You work by faith in Christ. Then rest by faith in him as well. Your tool is your *self*—keep it strong. What do you teach and believe about a Sabbath rest? As a wife, you can help your husband here. Do the two of you take a day off each week? Most ministers work six days each week, with extra time invested during the holidays. Maybe your weekly rhythm is contributing to your husband's lows. Fatigue feeds depression.[3]

Do not be a loner in ministry. Isolation, as well as fatigue, can contribute to depression. Ask God for another ministry couple with whom you can talk things through. Commit to meeting on a regular basis—weekly, or monthly, or quarterly. Walk in the light together (1 John 1:7), speaking the truth in love to each other, which "when each part is working properly, makes the body grow so that it builds itself up in love" (Ephesians 4:16).

If your husband cannot commit to regular meetings right now, seek out another ministry wife to meet with on your own. Is there a ministry wife you know of whom you respect? If not, contact your denominational office and ask for help in finding one. Pray over this new relationship and then connect with this older ministry wife and ask if you could treat her to a cup of coffee, or perhaps suggest meeting over FaceTime if she lives far from you. Let her know you are a younger ministry wife and you'd be honored if she would give you an hour to listen to your story and coach you at this stage of your ministry.

If things click during that first meeting, contact her again with a more extensive proposal, something that could work for both of you. Perhaps you'd like to meet once a month for six months and then reevaluate. Try not to overwhelm her. Have an end date in mind so she doesn't think she is commiting to a close relationship for her whole life! She might feel intimidated or underqualified. Let her know what you envision—perhaps sharing and prayer together, a chance to ask questions and gain encouragement from someone farther down the pathway of a ministry marriage. And then feel free to take the initiative. If she has agreed to talk with you once a month, text her with a simple, "Would you be free to talk sometime next week? If so, what works for you?" In other words, make her an offer she can't refuse! You both will benefit greatly.

Finally, seek the wisdom and understanding of a reputable Christian counselor if you or your husband sits in darkness for an extended time. There are loving servants of Christ trained to help you deal with the spiritual and emotional burdens you bear.

─────────── A LETTER TO YOUR PASTOR ───────────

Dear Pastor,

You have one of the most emotionally rich, but also demanding, jobs in the world. How are you doing emotionally? Do you experience a Monday morning adrenaline drain? Does it last longer than a day or two? Are you able to take a day off each week? Your wife really cares about that.

Ask her how she thinks you are doing. Then let her share her own inner condition. When is your next built-in recovery time? If you don't have one on your calendar, make a plan together.

Then think and pray together about another ministry couple you could befriend, with whom you can develop honest community.

From a recovering workaholic,

Jani

5

Help! I Can't Remember Their Names

DON'T WORRY. You're not the first and you won't be the last. In fact, to get into this elite pastor's wife club you need to take a vow that you won't break our record and be our first member to always remember everyone's name.

Forgetful Failure

You want to know all the people in your congregation. I know you do. After all, you wouldn't have a ministry without them! But with different people coming and going each week, it is almost impossible.

So just look that dear person straight in the eye, smile, and say, "Please forgive me. I'm trying to improve, but your name has just slipped out of my pea brain. I'm so sorry."

And when it happens with that same person again, just elaborate a little: "Please forgive me. I'm trying to improve, but I can't remember your name—again! I am so sorry and embarrassed."

Third time? Fake it. Or duck into the ladies' room and review your picture directory.

Then go home and forgive yourself.

The Importance of a Name

We're smiling together but mostly because we can identify. Names are important, especially to the name bearer.

My legal name is Jan. But my mother and my maternal grandmother used to call me Janny as a little girl. In high school some friends picked up on it, and for some reason they spelled it *Jani*, and it stuck. It is kind of a strange name, but my Ray calls me Jani, so that makes it music to my ears. People don't always know how to pronounce it, so I help them by saying, "Hi. My name is Jani. It rhymes with Annie, Granny, Fanny." And we have a good chuckle together.

Let's admit it. We want to know everyone's name in our church. We care about them. They are investing in us, and we are investing in them for eternity's sake. But sometimes, especially if your church is growing, it's just impossible to keep up with them all. Here are some things I've tried. Why not add your own ideas?

- I do hold myself responsible to know staff and officers' names and their families.

- I'm a visual learner, so I keep a list of new names I'm working on.

- At our new members' dinners in our home, I write out name tags for each guest and try to review them after they leave.

- I work on learning one new name a week, maybe the name of a parent whose children I teach in Sunday school, or the person who always sits three rows behind me and to my left.

There Is One Who Knows Every Name

There is someone who never forgets a name. Indeed, the name of each of his children is written in "the book of life" (see Daniel 12:1; Philippians 4:3; Revelation 20:15). So we can rejoice that their names are written in heaven (Luke 10:20) and ask God for help learning the names of those with whom we will spend eternity. It's important but not a pot to stew in time and time again. Do what you can, and then give yourself grace when you fail.

A LETTER TO YOUR PASTOR

Dear Pastor,

You might have more interactions with your people than your wife does. She needs your encouragement. As you share with your wife about your day, use names and give her connectors to help her remember those names. Be patient with her. Perhaps as a team you both could make a point of using people's names in conversations with church people, to help cover for each other.

From one who has trouble remembering,

Jani

6

Help! My Children
Aren't Perfect

YOUR HUSBAND'S MINISTRY PUTS you and your beloved children in the spotlight. The unintended but subtle pressures you feel to raise exemplary kids are real because families in our churches want hope for their own families. And if their pastor can't get it right, how can they?

A Glorious Advantage

Now, there is no guarantee that just because a child's parents are in ministry, the child will come to his or her own saving faith in Jesus Christ. But what a glorious advantage to grow up in a family where both parents love and serve the King of the universe. A child raised in the home of a godly couple wholeheartedly devoted to Christian ministry will meet people and have unique experiences that will shape his or her character for the years ahead.

Ray grew up as a pastor's kid, and he and his three grown siblings still love the Lord with all their hearts. Our own four children are now married and raising their own families. And we have the joy of watching each family "bearing fruit in every good work and increasing in the knowledge of God" (Colossians 1:10) while they "try to discern what is pleasing to the Lord" (Ephesians 5:10). Why do I share this with you, dear ministry wife? To give you hope that you too can begin a legacy of raising children who love the Lord, who raise children who love the Lord, who raise children who love the Lord—until Jesus returns.

How can I best encourage you? I want to lift burdens from you, not lay more on, because I remember how hard it can be. Someone once said that a couple raising young children is like running a day care with someone you used to date. How true!

I know there is nothing you long for more than to see Christ reigning as king in the hearts of your children. Let me humbly offer some principles we used while we were raising our kids. Maybe you'll get an idea or two that will encourage you as you raise your pastor's kids! I call these principles the "Three Ps for Parenting PKs."

Protect Your Pastor's Kids

All parents instinctively protect their children from busy streets, fire, and other dangers in their surroundings. But as a ministry wife, there is a unique danger you need to protect your child from—people's tongues.

In most churches, along with the courageous and compassionate children of God, you will also meet some people who fall into one of these three categories: the comparers, the critics, and the characters. You must protect your child from these dangerous types of people.

The comparers look back to the former days of your church and let you know that you and your children do not quite measure up to the previous pastor's family. "Pastor Smith's son could sit through the whole service without fidgeting. Every Sunday! I don't know how they got little Johnny to do it! Would you like me to give you Pastor Smith's contact information?" *Protect* your child from comparison. Let him know that the one you want him to imitate more than any person on earth is Jesus Christ. Let your child hear you clearly answer the question, "What's more important to your father and me? A child who can sit still in church (or meet any other unreasonable human expectation), or a child whose heart is sold out for Christ?"

The critics always have opinions about everything, opinions they feel obliged to tell you, sometimes in front of your children. Help your child to see that any opinion should be respectfully listened to and then judged on the basis of Scripture. Model this for them when you or your husband is criticized. Show your children how you can ask yourself, "Would it please God (Ephesians 5:10) for me to take this criticism to heart, to repent and change? Or is the criticism just an opportunity for this antagonist to vent a personal judgment on a sermon preached or a decision made that he or she disagrees with?" *Protect* your child from the critics by teaching them how to deal with criticism in a Christlike manner. Model how to listen respectfully, bring it to Jesus, and then decide how to respond.

The characters are those few people who don't understand how to build safe and relaxed relationships with other people. For whatever reason—whether background or upbringing, psychological or emotional difficulties, physical or spiritual afflictions—these are people who don't always make sense to your child. They may be sincere, Bible-believing, Jesus-loving people who truly don't process reality in a normal, reasonable way. Your child will need your advocacy here. Your family lives a very public life, which may feel like an invitation to some people to come in too close to your child. Do not allow it. *Protect* your child from any characters in your congregation by being vigilant to validate your child's natural distrust—or even fear—of some adults. Teach him that while he must be courteous, he does not need to engage with an adult who makes him feel uncomfortable. He can politely excuse himself and come find you.

It is your privilege to *protect* your child from the complainers and critics and characters in your church. Your husband will most often be too preoccupied to help you here. You *protect* your child by letting him know, through both your words and your actions, that he always comes before church members. Coach him in how to overlook—and even ignore—the pressures he will feel to act in certain ways because he is the pastor's kid. Talk with your child about Ecclesiastes 7:21: "Do not take to heart all the things that people say." Help him to see that his relationship with Jesus should govern his behavior more than his relationship with any church member.

Don't worry if your kids aren't perfect—just try to *protect* them from those who wish they were!

Persuade Your Pastor's Kids

First, *persuade your kids that they are more important* to you and their dad than any church member. Persuade them by proving it in your words and actions over and over again. Tell them, show them, and then show them again that they will always come before church members. Persuade them of their primary position in your heart and home and life story. Who cares, after all, if you and your husband develop an amazing ministry but lose your family along the way? Make it your goal to persuade your children of your overflowing love for them. That way it will be easier for each of your children to embrace God's personal and parental love for them as they grow (Psalm 103:13).

Ray's dad was a well-known pastor in Pasadena, California, where they moved when Ray was ten years old. Dad pastored a big church and bore many stresses as he cared for his large staff and growing congregation. But my Ray never wondered about his dad's love for him. Dad made sure he was there for Ray's football games, even coming to many of his practices!

A favorite way for Dad to persuade Ray of his love was to come check Ray out of school on an occasional Monday (Dad took Mondays off each week) so they could go body surfing together. It was an unexcused absence, but Dad didn't care, even when school authorities raised their eyebrows. His relationship with his son was more important. And it didn't seem to hurt Ray's educational success either. I'm married to a man who went on to earn two master's degrees and a doctorate.

You also need to *persuade your children to follow Christ with earnest and open hearts*. How do they see you living your life in the day-to-day, nitty-gritty details of building a home that delights in Christ? Is there joy in your home? Is there laughter? Do your kids like to be at home? What is the primary emotional atmosphere in your home? Is it anger? Tension? Or is there a Christlike peace and cheerfulness?

Part of persuasion is teaching and training. As you verbalize to your children why you require obedience and respect, let them live with a mother who obeys God cheerfully and quickly. Do they see you eagerly feeding on God's word even as you teach them to hide it in their young hearts? When you teach them to give part of their allowance to God's work, do they understand that you give cheerfully and regularly to God's work from your paycheck? Do they learn that God answers prayer through their prayer times with you?

Persuade your children by giving them biblical examples of other children who followed the Lord from a very young age, like Jehoash in 2 Kings 11–12 or Josiah in 2 Kings 22. Teach them that as a child learns to follow Christ early in life, it will be easier to "walk in a manner worthy of the Lord, fully pleasing to him" (Colossians 1:10) as they grow up (Proverbs 22:6).

Persuade your children that following Christ really is the best way to live. Talk much of the joys of knowing him today and the future joys awaiting all who love him. Introduce them either personally or through biographies to Christians who live with all-out abandon for Jesus Christ. Let them see the advantages of a life given fully to God. Share with your children "the glorious deeds of the LORD, and his might, and the wonders that he has done . . . so that they should set their hope in God" (Psalm 78:4, 7). Let them experience the wonder of a God who answers prayer and enters personally into the affairs of his children.

Finally, *persuade your children that ministry is a glorious privilege*. Let them hear from your own mouth how proud you are of their father for his hard work and passionate service for Christ. When your husband and you suffer in the ministry, your children are affected deeply, so let them see your steady resolve to identify with your suffering Savior as one worthy to follow no matter what! During the hard times, *persuade* your children that in Christ, our current reality is never our permanent reality. Assure them that God sees, he knows, he cares, and he is no man's debtor (Hebrews 6:10). He is real, and he is worth everything. He can be trusted in both the good and bad times, which they will surely face in their future as well.

Praise Your Pastor's Kids

What? Did you read that correctly?

Yes! *Praise* your kids. Let them know what treasures they are to you and what blessings they are going to be to their generation and the ones coming after them.

Affirm the good you see in them. Reward positive behavior. What if you were never praised for anything you did? What if your husband never noticed the delicious dinner you worked so hard to plan and prepare? What if your Bible study ladies never once let you know that your efforts were appreciated?

We made it a habit in our home to praise the lovely and good and true that we saw in our children. You, too, can praise your kids. To their faces. In front of their grandparents. To their father. In front of church members. Let them know what you think is special about each one. Thank them when they deserve it. And sometimes a little reward with that praise will reinforce that good behavior even more deeply.

Let me close this chapter by assuring you that it is perfect that your children *aren't* perfect! What your flock really needs to see is a family serving God with wholehearted devotion while dealing with the realities of sinful parents raising sinful children in this broken and confusing world. Your authenticity and vulnerability will be a more productive tool for Christ than any perfectly behaved child.

Don't be afraid of the pressures. Absorb them for Christ's sake. He loves your children even more than you do.

———————— A LETTER TO YOUR PASTOR ————————

Dear Pastor,

Your children are more precious to you than even your ministry. Ask your wife how she thinks each of your kids is doing. Your conversation could include:

- *Do your children feel protected from the inevitable criticisms of church members?*
- *How is each child doing in his progress toward claiming Christ as his own Savior and King?*
- *Is the home you are building filled with encouragement and fun as well as order and discipline?*

- *How often do your children hear you say you're proud of them and you delight in them?*

Now, why not get down on your knees together and pray for your children?

It will be worth it all,

Jani

7

Help! My Pastor Doesn't Understand Me

NO ONE EVER INTENDS to end up in a mediocre marriage, and yet look around you. We live in a day of impoverished marriages—weak in purpose, scorning the scriptural obligations of sustained fidelity, and deprived of real, lifelong romance.

A Complex Mystery

What do you want most from your marriage? What would make it deeply satisfying for both you and your husband?

To get there, you need to enter in wholeheartedly to this lifetime commitment and teach your husband how to love you in meaningful ways. Why? Because he's a man and you're a woman. That combination is a complex mystery, full of both wonder and bewilderment.

Don't be hurt if your husband doesn't yet know how to love you in ways that are meaningful to you. Don't be crushed if he can't yet understand who you really are as a woman. Be his teacher in gentle, flirtatious ways, and then be grateful that he's learning how to love a woman—you!

Help Him Learn How to Love You Emotionally

Imagine this scene: "Dearly beloved, we are gathered here together in the sight of God and these witnesses to join this man and this woman together in holy matrimony and to see just how much pain these two can cause each other and their families in the years ahead."

We smile, and yet who hasn't been touched by marital pain, either in our own marriage or in the marriage of someone we hold dear to our heart? Ministry marriages are not exempt. We all face struggles this side of heaven.

When I'm going through a hard time, my tendency is to withdraw from Ray. "Is something bothering you?" Ray will ask when I give him the silent treatment.

"No!" I tell him because I'm not ready to talk about it yet.

"Really? Are you sure?" he will gently try again to draw me out.

"Yes, I'm just fine!" I will snip at him, which being translated means, "I'm upset, and I feel guilty about being upset, and we've talked about this before, and it hasn't worked, and I don't want to bring it up again, and I'm afraid I'll have to live my whole life with this issue unresolved! So it's just easier to withdraw in fear and defeat. But please don't let me stay here too long. I need your help. I'm really not okay."

Dr. John Gottman says there are three ways to relate to another person:

1. Turn toward—this is positive, courteous, gentle.
2. Turn against—this is mean, argumentative, sarcastic.
3. Turn away—we ignore, or act as if we are preoccupied.[4]

For a deeper level of emotional intimacy and understanding, we need to develop a habit of turning toward our husband. I believe the reason we turn against or away from our husband *is not* that we don't want comfort. We just don't want the kind of comfort we've been offered in the past.

Generally, Ray has tried to comfort me with words. If he can reason out *why* something happened, then it will be okay. He often tries to solve it logically so that it won't happen again. I, however, more often need gestures—hugs, flowers, help with the children or house. I've had to think through and then try to teach Ray how best to comfort me. What will help? What will hinder? Through the years, it has been profoundly rewarding as we have learned the best ways to turn toward each other.

Ray and I enjoy watching those old black-and-white romance movies. She always has just the right words to say, and he always knows exactly what to do. Well, she has a script giving her the words to say, and he has a director telling him what to do! So, dear wife, join me in gently becoming your husband's director.

Let me illustrate from a scene at the Ortlund household, eight years into our marriage. We had four children, and the first three came in less than three years. Ray was on full-time staff at a large church in California, as well as teaching Greek two evenings a week, while also working on a second master's degree from the University of California at Berkeley. How we ever had time for making three babies, I still can't figure out! I was struggling to keep my head above water with my responsibilities as a ministry wife and mother.

After dinner on the evenings when Ray was home, he would help me bathe and read to the kids, and then we'd tuck them into their cribs or bed in the little room the three of them shared. Sounds pretty great, doesn't it? But it wasn't enough for Jani! After the kids were down, I would go to clean up the kitchen while Ray sat down to read. Somehow my sinful heart was envious that he had the luxury of sitting down while I still had work to finish. So I would bang those dishes around, hoping he would get a hint. He didn't. Finally, one night while I banged the pots and pans as loudly as I could, I started crying, and he came out to see what was wrong. I told him through my tears how jealous I was of his freedom to sit and read in peace, while also acknowledging feeling guilty about it. "Darling," he said, "Why didn't you just ask me to help you? I had no idea. I want to bless you and love you well." Somehow I wanted him to figure out my needs without my coaching him. It seemed less romantic if I had to ask for help. Silly, ignorant me!

But what young marriage, especially if there are little people demanding your constant attention, doesn't need some coaching? Don't be afraid to tenderly teach your husband how to love you. Where else can he learn these kinds of strategies?

If You Don't

If you don't teach him how to love you emotionally, there will be at least two negative outcomes:

1. He will probably never learn, and then you'll turn to other sources for comfort—your mom, friends, food, escapist novels and films, the Internet, etc.
2. Your son will never see up close how a man can comfort his wife, and your daughter will never learn how to communicate her needs in absorbable ways to the man of her dreams.

Teach your husband how to turn toward you. Turning toward someone says, "I hear you; I'm interested in you; I understand you; I'm on your side; I'd like to help you." It is not wrong to ask. David asked God to turn toward him: "Turn to me and be gracious to me, for I am lonely and afflicted" (Psalm 25:16).

Try to use words before the tears start flowing. "I feel valued when you help me with the dishes after you invited company over for dinner." "I feel heard when you remember to pick up the milk that I emailed you about." Thank him. Reward him!

You are building a solid, long-term relationship with which to bless your children and your church. Don't attack and withdraw. Men and women have distinct preferences regarding sex, responsibilities, adventure, and friendship. Let your differences be a source of pride and intrigue rather than resentment and bitterness. Choose to celebrate your differences, not bemoan them. Embrace both your femininity and his masculinity.

Let's not be men bashers! Guard against a hardness of heart. Jesus said in Mark 10:4–5 that Moses allowed for divorce because of our hardness of heart. Pray for a soft heart. Our kind King has *never once not answered* this prayer for me: "Lord, I don't have warm feelings for my man today. Soften my heart toward him. Increase my love for him. Please help me be a channel of your favor upon him."

Take the Long-Term Approach

Help your husband learn how to meet your emotional needs. Take the long-term approach. Don't give up too soon! Forgiving your husband when he doesn't understand you means giving him the freedom to be an imperfect human being, which we all are!

And those needs he can't meet or won't meet or just keeps forgetting to meet—bring those needs to your heavenly Husband. Give yourself up to God as Christ did. "Walk in love, as Christ loved us and gave himself up for us, a fragrant offering and sacrifice to God" (Ephesians 5:2). Release those unmet needs as a fragrant offering to the God who allows some earthly needs to go unmet for reasons beyond our comprehension. Trust the creator of marriage, the one who brought you and your husband together, with those confusing, and even painful parts of your marriage, remembering that "he rewards those who seek him" (Hebrews 11:6).

———— A LETTER TO YOUR PASTOR ————

Dear Pastor,

Your wife has emotional needs that she may be embarrassed or even unable to communicate to you. She needs your patience. Prove to her your desire to live with her in an understanding way by using words like, "I hear you. I'm interested in you. You are a delightful mystery I want to spend my life understanding and enjoying."

And then invite her to help you do some good detective work!

Because you have a mystery worth exploring,

Jani

8

Help! I Haven't Seen
Them for a While

IT'S NOT A UNIQUE EXPERIENCE, but it still stings.[5] It starts
with a simple Sunday afternoon question from your husband:
"Have you seen Bill and Betty lately?"

"No, I haven't seen them for a while, have you?"

You both realize that they have been MIW ("Missing in Worship") the past few Sundays. Over coffee the following week,
they tell you that they have decided to try a different church.

What Happened?

What? Where did that come from? Why? How? You search your
conscience and calendar trying to understand what happened.
This was a couple you invested in so deeply. They shared many
meals around your table. You hosted a baby shower for her little
one. You met with them when they were suffering and sat in
the waiting room when he had surgery. You promised to pray
when they had a need, and you did. You brought meals over

when they were sick. You enjoyed giving them Christmas and birthday gifts and sometimes even shared holidays together. You built bridges for them in your congregation and offered them meaningful ways to serve Christ among your members. And you envisioned a loving friendship stretching far into the future.

Then they slipped away with barely a goodbye. You feel the loss and rejection. You also feel the guilt of somehow failing them, and perhaps even the Lord Jesus. Sadness seeps in when you think about them. You see them from afar on social media and wonder how they are. Her birthday comes around—should you send her a card? You even begin to wonder if you have the courage to keep opening your home and heart to others.

Has this ever happened to you? If not yet, it will. How can we as ministry wives keep cheerfully serving the people God brings to us despite all the bumps and bruises along the way?

Listen to Jesus

First, listen to Jesus instead of muttering to yourself. Don't waste your spiritual and emotional energy, which is limited to begin with, fussing within your own head. Let Jesus speak to your heart. Is he speaking words of conviction? Are there ways he wants you to change? If so, then by his grace do it. Immediately.

But if he is not—if, as you search the Bible, you do not hear his words of personal, sacred conviction as you try to explain this loss—then ask him to help you lift these friends up to him as an offering, a sacrifice of service to your Savior, to do with whatever he deems best.

Through him then let us continually offer up a sacrifice of praise to God, that is, the fruit of lips that acknowledge his name. Do not neglect to do good and to share what you have, for such sacrifices are pleasing to God. (Hebrews 13:15–16)

Look to Jesus

Fix your eyes on Jesus. Imitate him. He came to serve, not to be served. His life was an offering to his Father to do with as he pleased. Jesus gave all of himself, knowing even before he offered his very life that there would be pain and loss and rejection in the offering. And he calls us to follow him. "So you also, when you have done all that you were commanded, say, 'We are unworthy servants; we have only done what was our duty'" (Luke 17:10).

He understands. Look to Jesus. He is able to sympathize with our weaknesses. As we draw near to the throne of grace, we will "receive mercy and find grace to help in time of need" (Hebrews 4:16).

Live for Jesus

Let your life be a sacrifice to our King. He is worthy of any and all effort. He is no man's debtor. You serve the one who will not "overlook your work and the love that you have shown for his name in serving the saints, as you still do" (Hebrews 6:10).

The time you invest, he sees. The money you spend, he values. The love you offer, he counts as love offered to him. Let's encourage each other to minister with open hands— open hands that lovingly welcome people, open hands that generously serve them, and open hands that release them without bitterness. All ministry is an open-handed offering to him, and "in the Lord your labor is not in vain" (1 Corinthians 15:58).

--------- A LETTER TO YOUR PASTOR ---------

Dear Pastor,

Chances are, your church has experienced the loss of a wonderful family for no apparent reason. Your wife may feel their departure from your congregation even more keenly than you do. She might struggle with hurt, or loneliness, or even some unnecessary guilt over their leaving.

Ask her to share with you how she is doing. Talk through how you can process these losses in a biblical and healthy way. Your understanding can do much to heal that wound in her heart.

In the trenches with you,

Jani

9

Help! I Need More of God

SOME PEOPLE EXPECT the pastor's wife to have the most ideal and perfect relationship with God. After all, she lives with the pastor, sleeps with him, has ready access to help for any questions or problems that arise, right?

Ah, now that's a laugh! We all know that a pastor's schedule, his energy level, and his own personal needs prevent a pastor's wife from relying solely on her husband to feed her spiritually.

What should we—women married to men in ministry—do to stay spiritually radiant? How can God's redeeming love fill our hearts in such a way that we begin to live outside our own needs, gladly giving ourselves to his eternal purposes in our marriage and family, our church and community?

Feeding Your Soul

One way—I believe *the most important way*—is to spend time daily with our Redeemer. Meeting regularly with Jesus is necessary if we want to enjoy and support vibrant spiritual health. Just as physical food feeds our bodies the Bible is food for our souls.

We need time every day in the word; otherwise, our souls will stagnate and settle into a malnourished subsistence that slowly starts to feel normal. If we are not feeding our hearts and minds with eternal, heavenly food, our souls will shrink for lack of nourishment.

Think of all we feed our bodies and minds. Think of the time you spent just this past week on food shopping and meal prepping, on eating and cleaning up, on working, on housekeeping and child minding, on reading and surfing the Internet, on exercising and watching TV and playing games on your phone. Now compare that to the time you spent in nearness to God through prayer and Bible study, meditation and memorization. It's not easy, is it? There is so much we must do in this life, along with all we want to do!

But in order to support our husband in meaningful ways, we need to be supported ourselves with an all-powerful heavenly support. We need daily refreshment and encouragement from which we can draw as we seek to love our pastor well. The best and most satisfying way to get that refreshment is by going deep into God's word in study and meditation and spending regular time in prayer. We need to feast on the abundance of his house and let him give us drink from his river of delights (Psalm 36:8).

What things are *precious* to you? Is God's love *precious* to you? Can you say with David, "How precious is your steadfast love, O God!" (Psalm 36:7)? Maybe you feel far from God's love these days. Ask him to reignite and increase your love for him as you read this chapter. "Will you not revive us again, that your people may rejoice in you?" (Psalm 85:6).

David tells us that God's love is steadfast. What does that mean? It means that God's precious love is constant and steady. It can be depended upon. It is unfailing. His love never falters. He fixes his love upon us with clear, unchangeable intent.

We can count on God's love. Human love is very fragile, as many of us know from personal experience. Some of us have been deeply hurt by people we thought we could love and trust who in the end proved unfaithful. But God's love will *never* falter or waver.

> The LORD is good;
>> his steadfast love endures forever,
>> and his faithfulness to all generations. (Psalm 100:5)

> The steadfast love of the LORD never ceases;
>> his mercies never come to an end;
> they are new every morning;
>> great is your faithfulness. (Lamentations 3:22–23)

> Return to the LORD your God,
>> for he is gracious and merciful,
> slow to anger, and abounding in steadfast love. (Joel 2:13)

What do you abound in? Complaints? Fatigue? Fears? Housework? Bills?

Snuggle in Close to His Heart

Life can be scary. Ministry can be scary. But there is a place where those who know God through Christ can find shelter and relief from anything that this world assaults them with, a place where God's precious, steadfast love is abundant.

Where is that place? David describes it as in the shadow of God's wings:

> How precious is your steadfast love, O God!
> The children of mankind take refuge in the shadow of
> your wings. (Psalm 36:7)

To be in the shadow of someone's wings means coming near; it hints at snuggling in close to the heart. There is a sanctuary that God opens up to anyone who dares to draw near to him. He spreads out his wings and invites us to nestle in close to his heart. It is there that God offers you a love that will never let you go. He secures within your soul an eternal love, and nothing can ever wrench you out of his loving embrace.

In the New Testament Paul puts it this way: "Who shall separate us from the love of Christ? Shall tribulation, or distress, or persecution, or famine, or nakedness, or danger, or sword? . . . For I am sure that neither death nor life, nor angels nor rulers, nor things present nor things to come, nor powers, nor height nor depth, nor anything else in all creation, will be able to separate us from the love of God in Christ Jesus our Lord" (Romans 8:35–39).

It's as if Paul is saying, "Imagine the worst scenario possible. Do you think God's love can remain credible even there?" Dear sister, *nothing* can separate you from the love of God through Christ Jesus. Not problems at church or your failures or your husband's failures, not your sins or someone else's sins against you, and not even your indifferent or dry spirit. Nothing will ever be able to separate you from his love. That is his promise, and we serve the God who always keeps his promises.

The Most Fulfilling Romance of All

What God wants us to see through his holy word to us is that our lives are a love story. Our sufferings and our failings do not define us; the precious, steadfast love of God defines us. Our redemption is the most beautiful love story ever told. Relish it. Live your life out of an inner fullness. Don't live from the outside in—live from the inside out. Always start with God and his fullness. You are loved with a love so vast that it will take all eternity to experience it.

God made the human heart. He created your heart for worship. Worship is more than going to church or singing hymns or praying. To worship means to give your heart away to something. Will you give your heart away in deeper abandon to God even today as you read?

You are engaged to Christ now. Your earthly death will be your wedding day. He is courting you now—winning your heart through his precious steadfast love. Keep responding to him in these courtship days as you wait for that glorious heavenly wedding. Open your heart again to Christ right now. He knows you best and loves you most. Let the precious, steadfast love of God flood your life with a deep beauty and a new spiritual radiance.

We often come to God thinking we're making a covenant with him. That is part of it, but your salvation is much larger than that. Within the triune Godhead, God made a decision with Christ about you—about me. Christ effected it on the cross, and the Holy Spirit sealed it with his very presence in your innermost heart.

Relish your redemption. Make your relationship with your heavenly Father the most important one in your whole life.

Show it by your schedule and bank account and conversations and relationships. Refresh and renew your commitment to Jesus Christ. Feast on the abundance of his house and let him give you drink from his river of delights as you take refuge in the shadow of his wings.

You Are Your Habits

I know it is hard to establish this daily pattern, but don't miss out any longer. You are your habits! So let's develop the gloriously blessed habit of spending time with God each day.

Every human being has twenty-four hours each day to get things done. I want to encourage you here. When I first started meeting daily with the Lord, I kept waiting for it to get easier. When I was a student, I thought it would be easier when I got a regular job with set hours. When I began teaching school, I thought it would become easier once I was able to stay at home and develop my own schedule. And when I was home with my babies, I just knew it would be easier when they started sleeping through the night. As they grew, I thought ahead to the years when I would be free from all the responsibilities of raising these kids. You get the point—I just kept waiting, hoping. Now I finally realize that although meeting daily with the Lord has not necessarily gotten easier, it has gotten so much better! Every year we have spent sweet time together, and he has helped me to increase in my knowledge of him and his ways. This holy habit is one I never want to change.

Truly, there is no big secret to developing this habit. There is a story of a seminary president who was known to get up very early each morning to meet with God. A student was encouraged by others to ask the president if he would be willing to share his secret for getting up so early. Imagine the student's surprise when the president reportedly said, "Secret? Why, of course I'll share it with you! I set my alarm—*and then I get up.*"

We need to build for tomorrow today! That is the only way the wisdom and help and guidance will be there when we need it. We need to plan for this time. We need to be strong and courageous enough to fight for it, to claw for it, to make it happen. Don't develop your time with Christ around your schedule; develop your schedule around your time with Christ.

Jesus showed us the way:

> They went into Capernaum, and immediately on the Sabbath he entered the synagogue and was teaching. And they were astonished at his teaching, for he taught them as one who had authority, and not as the scribes. And immediately there was in their synagogue a man with an unclean spirit. And he cried out, "What have you to do with us, Jesus of Nazareth? Have you come to destroy us? I know who you are—the Holy One of God." But Jesus rebuked him, saying, "Be silent, and come out of him!" And the unclean spirit, convulsing him and crying out with a loud voice, came out of him. And they were all amazed, so that they questioned among themselves, saying, "What is this? A new teaching with authority! He commands even the unclean spirits, and they obey him." And at once his fame spread everywhere throughout all the surrounding region of Galilee.
>
> And immediately he left the synagogue and entered the house of Simon and Andrew, with James and John. Now Simon's mother-in-law lay ill with a fever, and immediately

they told him about her. And he came and took her by the hand and lifted her up, and the fever left her, and she began to serve them.

That evening at sundown they brought to him all who were sick or oppressed by demons. And the whole city was gathered together at the door. And he healed many who were sick with various diseases, and cast out many demons. And he would not permit the demons to speak, because they knew him. (Mark 1:21–34)

We see in this passage that Jesus taught in the synagogue, rebuked an evil spirit, entered Simon and Andrew's house, and healed Simon's mother-in-law and many who were sick or oppressed by demons, and then finally at sundown the whole city came and gathered together at the door to see him. What a full day! Notice what comes next. Jesus went out early the next morning to meet with his Father:

And rising very early in the morning, while it was still dark, he departed and went out to a desolate place, and there he prayed. And Simon and those who were with him searched for him, and they found him and said to him, "Everyone is looking for you." (Mark 1:35–37).

We can see a similar example in Luke 5:15–16. If Jesus withdrew to spend time with his Father, how much more should we!

Two Questions We Can Ask When We Meet with the Lord
Perhaps some of you aren't sure what to do during your times with the Lord. Or you've tried it in the past and have been frustrated, maybe even bored. And then you feel so guilty! Let's

look at Paul's first personal meeting with the Lord and find two questions we can bring to our meeting with Jesus.

Look at Acts 22, where Paul (back when he was still called "Saul") is on the road to Damascus. You'll see in verses 8 and 10 the questions Paul asked the Lord during this first meeting with Jesus: "Who are you, Lord?" and "What shall I do, Lord?"

These are great biblical questions to ask any time you are meeting with God. I suggest you put those two questions at the top of a piece of paper, along with the date and the Bible verses you are reading. Then read and spend some time trying to answer one or both questions from your passage. You may want to keep your notes for future reference—either for your own edification or as a stimulus for when you share from a passage of Scripture.

Whatever you do, open your heart anew to Christ. Confess any boredom or indifference. Ask, seek, and knock, and he promises to answer and open a way for you to receive good gifts from his heavenly Father (Matthew 7:7–11). Do not starve yourself any longer.

———————— A LETTER TO YOUR PASTOR ————————

Dear Pastor,

Your wife may be struggling spiritually but is afraid to talk to anyone about it—maybe even you. Gently ask her how she is doing way down deep in her soul. Does she feel the loving nearness of her heavenly Father? Most of her friends will assume that she is a spiritual giant because she's married to you!

How can you help her draw nearer to Christ? Can you give her time away from the kids so she can slip away to meet with her Lord? Maybe she would enjoy getting together with you once a week for Bible reading or prayer. Or how about freeing her for a weekend away for spiritual refreshment while you manage the home front? Care for your wife as you do your flock. She needs the Lord too.

That we may present everyone mature in Christ,

Jani

10

Help! Our Romance
Is Regressing

I BELIEVE THAT THE HAPPY responsibility of every pastor's wife is to seduce her pastor.

God Is Pro-Romance

Yes, you read that correctly! A husband's strongest safeguard against adultery is a fun and fulfilling relationship with his wife. We as Christian leaders should have the happiest, most romantic and satisfying marriages in all of society.

God's word is unashamedly pro-romance. He made us male and female as part of his "very good" creation. Think of all the love stories in the Bible: Abraham and Sarah, Isaac and Rebekah, Jacob and Rachel, Ruth and Boaz, along with others. Think of some of the biblical passages that are erotic, such as the Song of Solomon or Proverbs 5:15–19. God celebrates love and sex in marriage. He values our sexuality and calls for us to enjoy this beautiful gift within the security of a lifelong marital commitment. Let's love our husband in all the ways God encourages us to.

You Marry Three Men

Happily married women know that having a husband does not make a great marriage, any more than having a piano makes a great musician. You see, you really marry three men:

1. The man you thought you married.
2. The man he really is.
3. And the man he is becoming by being married to you.

What will your husband become because he chose *you*? Are you helping him to be a one-woman man?

There are many attractions outside of your marriage that can divide you and your husband. A strong, romantic, happy marriage is a sure defense against many of the evil forces that want to see your man defeated. In a ministry marriage, it is vital to refresh your romance, and then come back and refresh it again, and to keep on refreshing it until your earthly marriage comes to its conclusion and you see each other off to your heavenly, eternal union with Christ.

A Soft Spot in Your Marriage

You, dear ministry wife, are the only legal and God-blessed source of sexual fulfillment that your pastor has as he follows the Lord carefully. My husband shares so much with others—his time, his energies, his money, his wisdom, his humor, his library, even his venison! But there is one thing he never shares with anyone else—it is mine alone—and that is his body. I want to treasure this gift.

Learn to give your husband the joy and pleasure that he can experience only within the security of a godly marriage. Proverbs 5:15–19 tells your husband to rejoice in you, to be delightfully satisfied with your breasts, to be intoxicated by your love. Are you doing all you can to be as captivating as possible? Do you still flirt with him? Have you ever seduced your husband?

If the physical side of your marriage doesn't become all it can be, your marriage can still survive because sex isn't everything. But your marriage will have a soft spot, a vulnerable side where Satan can attack. So seek to cultivate a deep physical intimacy with your husband that binds his heart and his body to yours. This takes time, creativity, and initiative. Don't give up too soon. Mom Ortlund used to tell me, "Good things take time before they become good."

You may need help here. I sure did! I just didn't understand the intricacies of the sexual delights God offers to a married couple. In the early years of our marriage, Ray enjoyed our times of intimacy more than I did. I needed to educate myself and coach Ray as well. A book that has greatly helped us is Ed and Gaye Wheat's *Intended for Pleasure: Sex Technique and Sexual Fulfillment in Christian Marriage*.[6] We have found it very enlightening, and we often give a copy as a shower or wedding gift to young couples. Get a copy and read it. Share it with your husband. I think you'll enjoy some happy results!

A Challenge for You

Let me challenge you. By the time you finish this book, plan one surprise for your husband. You probably would rather have him initiate, but I encourage you to try it and see what happens.

- Buy that negligee that only he sees and plan a special night together.

- Splurge on a roomful of candles and some new perfume—and then use them.

- Arrange a dinner at home with no children and see where it might lead. (May I recommend it not be on a night where his favorite sports team is playing in a finals competition? Just a little motherly advice.)

- A personal favorite of mine is to surprise Ray for lunch. Once I was so lonely for time with my man that I asked one of our elders, who had a monthly lunch meeting with Ray, if I could possibly take his place as a special surprise. He graciously agreed. Then I called Ray's assistant and had her block out extra time for our lunch, asking her to play along with me. You can imagine Ray's smile when he walked into the hotel restaurant and discovered that *I* was his lunch business meeting. We had such fun together! And, believe me, that was nothing compared to Ray's response when the waitress cleared away his plate, and there was a room key waiting for us. We still smile over that unique tête-à-tête.

- Create a secret connection with each other as this couple did in the story below.

Last weekend we celebrated my parents' fiftieth wedding anniversary. This morning they left on a long awaited trip to Hawaii. They were as excited as if it were their honeymoon. When my parents married, they had only enough money for a three-day trip fifty miles from home. They made a pact that each time they made love, they would put a dollar in a special metal box and save it for a honeymoon in Hawaii for their fiftieth anniversary. Dad was a policeman, and Mom was a schoolteacher. They lived in a modest house and did all their own repairs. Raising five children was a challenge, and sometimes, money was short. But no matter what emergency came up, Dad would not let Mom take any money out of the "Hawaii account." As the account grew, they put it in a savings account and then bought CDs.

My parents were always very much in love. I can remember Dad's coming home and telling Mom, "I have a dollar in my pocket," and she would smile at him and reply, "I know how to spend it."

When each of us children married, Mom and Dad gave us a small metal box and told us their secret, which we found enchanting. All five of us are now saving for our dream honeymoon. Mom and Dad never told us how much money they had managed to save, but it must have been considerable because when they cashed in those CDs, they had enough for airfare to Hawaii plus hotel accommodations for ten days and plenty of spending money. As they told us good-bye before leaving, Dad winked and said, "Tonight we are starting an account for Cancun. That should only take twenty-five years!"[7]

Will you accept my challenge? Oh, please do! Ministry marriages bear unique strains. But God can use those very strains to build a biblical romance that not only thrills and satisfies you, but also blesses the lives of those who know you. Embrace

God's call to love your husband in ways that only you can. Seek to build an extended, authentic, unbroken love affair with that pastor you're married to.

Now, dear sister, put down this book and begin a plan of action! You'll both be glad you did.

A LETTER TO YOUR PASTOR

Dear Pastor,

I've given your wife an assignment to help you obey Proverbs 5:15–19 by being as captivating as she can be. I've encouraged her to coach you in how to love her physically in all those satisfying ways that only you can. I've urged her to help your marriage become all that God wants it to be.

Are you willing to assist her in completing this assignment? I can assure you, it's one you'll be happy to work on together!

May God bless your romance more and more,

Jani

11

Help! They're Talking Again

THE EMAIL WAS NEW, but, sadly, the emotional trauma was not:

> Dear Jani,
> My husband has been publicly slandered and betrayed by
> our closest friends who were on staff with us until we got
> fired. It is destroying my faith. With no job and no income
> for months now, I don't know how to move on some days.
> Going forward in ministry again is confusing—we have such
> a huge lack of trust and are severely wounded. How do you
> keep from dying? How do you move on from the hurt and
> betrayal? How do you make sense of this with God and his
> sovereignty?

How, indeed?

The Topic of Many Conversations

Leaders are talked about. By virtue of his position, your husband will be the subject of many conversations. And some of that talk will find its way back to you. As women in ministry, and as daughters of the King, we need to think through how to deal with the inevitable criticism and gossip that unfortunately circulate in our culture today, even within our Christian culture.

We know that truth stabilizes and strengthens relationships. That's why God lovingly forbids every kind of falsehood (Exodus 20:16; Leviticus 19:11). He instructs us to make truth, purity, and honor the foundation of all our relationships.

But we find this so hard! We are liars by nature and live in a culture of lies. Paul had to tell the Colossian Christians, "Do not lie to one another, seeing that you have put off the old self" (Col. 3:9). We could all tell stories of rumors or lies or half-truths—or even times when the truth was just withheld—and how this brought deep pain and ultimately poisoned relationships in our lives.

Your Tongue

Let's think through, first, our responsibility in this area. James 3 speaks of the tongue being such a small part of our body yet revealing how well we control our whole body: "If anyone does not stumble in what he says, he is . . . able also to bridle his whole body. . . . But no human being can tame the tongue. It is a restless evil, full of deadly poison" (vv. 2, 8).

How we need God's help here as leaders in his work! Francis Schaeffer's wife, Edith, put it this way:

> If a report is unnecessary and unkind, and might just be a little exaggerated in the retelling of it the next time, we'd better be silent about it. It is my tongue and your tongue that is likened to a bucking horse that is running away with its rider. It is my tongue and yours that is likened to the ship

tossing on the waves with the rudder not properly in the hands of the expert.[8]

Once spoken, any word of gossip—indeed any word we ever speak—is impossible to retrieve. You might just as well try to capture a cloud. Maybe you've heard the story of the young monk who went to his superior because he had sinned in how he had spoken about someone. His superior instructed him to go put a feather on the doorstep of all those he had spoken to about this matter, which the young monk immediately did. He returned to his superior to ask what he should do next. When his superior told him he must now go and retrieve each feather, he exclaimed, "But I can't! By now those feathers are spread all over town!" His superior's quiet response was, "Likewise your words." As leaders, let's plead with God to: "Set a guard, O LORD, over my mouth; keep watch over the door of my lips!" (Psalm 141:3).

We must do all we can to see that honesty, kindness, and love govern the speech in our spheres of influence—in our homes, our bedrooms, around our breakfast tables, in our phone conversations and emails. "Gracious words are like a honeycomb, sweetness to the soul and health to the body" (Proverbs 16:24). Do my words taste sweet and bring health to those who hear them? "Death and life are in the power of the tongue" (Proverbs 18:21). Is my speech life-giving or life-draining?

Someone Else's Tongue

You may be thinking, "Jani, it's not my own tongue that's the problem here. Although the Lord has dealt with me before regarding my tongue, my tears and fears today are not about my own words. It's the rumors that others have spread about me and my loved ones that hurt so much. The pain of their criticism goes deep down into my heart. It also has long-lasting effects on our family."

A cell phone can be as deadly as a gun. I've been there. I've experienced the disbelief and panicky pain of another's loose tongue, along with the irreversible ramifications for ministry that slander brings on. How would I counsel you?

Let Your Light Shine

In the first place, let's live such Christ-filled lives that when anything false is said about us, others will have numerous good reasons not to believe it. "Give no offense to Jews or to Greeks or to the church of God, just as I try to please everyone in everything I do" (1 Corinthians 10:32–33). Ask God to help you sparkle with his radiance, shedding his resplendent light on every person you interact with (Matthew 5:16).

Never *About*—Always *To*

We have a rule in our home. It was a rule that Amy Carmichael, missionary to orphans in India, established as she led her ministry: "Never *about*—always *to*." Let's ask ourselves and others, "Have you talked to that person directly before sharing something about him or her? Is her name safe in your house?"

In one of our pastorates, during a difficult time, a staff member resigned but came back a few months later and asked Ray to forgive him for spreading lies about Ray. Of course, Ray did forgive him. But the damage had been done, and the man made no effort to undo that damage. We are still living with repercussions from the slander. I am not saying this because our experience was so unusual but because it was so common—as you know, I am sure. And here is my point: if only he had talked *to* Ray rather than *about* him.

Look to Other Christ-Filled Leaders

I've found it helpful to study other Christian leaders who have endured grievous criticism and outlandish attacks on their reputations and to learn from their examples. I recommend reading good Christian biographies to see how others responded. Sarah Edwards, Charles Simeon, Amy Carmichael—there are plenty to choose from because slander has always been pervasive among us. Instead of wasting emotional energy defending and protecting themselves, you will see how they turned to God. And that is what we must do too. "Consider the outcome of their way of life, and imitate their faith" (Hebrews 13:7).

The Bible says that love covers over an offense (Proverbs 17:9). Part of ministry is learning to cover over the offenses of others with Christian love. What does this look like? George MacDonald shows us in his insightful book *Malcolm*. Malcolm had been unjustly accused of wrongdoing, and rumors were spreading. Here Malcolm is talking with his very wise older friend, Miss Horn:

> "Well, mem, what would you have me do? I can't send my old daddy around the town with his pipes to proclaim that I'm not the man. I'm thinking I'll just have to leave the place." . . .
>
> "Many a better man has been called worse, and folk soon forget that ever the lie was said. No, no; never run from a lie. And never say, neither, that you didn't do the thing, except

it be laid straight to your face. Let a lie lay in the dirt. If you pick it up, the dirt'll stick to you, even if you fling the lie over the dike at the end of the world. No, no! Let a lie lay as you would the devil's tail!"

"What should I do then, mem?"

"Do? Who said you was to do anything? The best doing is to stand still. Let the wave wash over you without ducking. . . . Go your way, laddie; say your prayers, and hold up your head. Who wouldn't rather be accused of all the sins of the Commandments than to be guilty of one of them?"[9]

Go to Christ

Dear sister, there is more to being a Christian than asking Jesus into your heart. Belief in his goodness and watch care and love for you will have its full effect only when you *feel* loved and cared for from your heart in the midst of your own real life. All behavior is rooted in what we believe. Our emotions stem from our heartfelt belief that either:

Jesus is enough

or

Jesus is not enough (and we must somehow fill the void we're feeling that he can't or won't fill for us).

For instance, if I say I believe that God cares about me and is sovereign over my whole life in mercy and love, yet I am held captive by various paralyzing and Christ-dishonoring fears, I don't *really* trust that God is good. My belief in his sovereign control is only an intellectual concept, not a heartfelt belief.

When I stop trusting God, I start forging my own way, and then I become very dangerous. After all, the devils believe in God (James 2:19). But they aren't in a love relationship with God—and that makes all the difference. Our hearts need to be renewed and thrilled with God's redeeming love.

Remember Psalm 36:7–9:

> How precious is your steadfast love, O God!
> > The children of mankind take refuge in the shadow of
> > > your wings.
> They feast on the abundance of your house,
> > and you them give drink from the river of your
> > > delights.
> For with you is the fountain of life;
> > in your light do we see light.

It is God's love that redeems our lives from the pit, not a person's high regard for us or a perfect reputation. So when we're stung, or set back, or even fired, because of gossip and rumor, we come to the God who is redeeming all of our lives, not just at the point of conversion, but all along the way as we stumble toward heaven in our weaknesses.

As God fulfills his promise of grace in us, we will feel so humbled by his saving love for us that we won't allow slander and criticism to derail us emotionally or spiritually. Humility—true humility—defuses rumors. To be truly humble means that I am shocked at nothing that someone might say about me, because if they knew me better they would have even more to talk about.

Not only will God's grace fill us with humility, but we will become so deeply secure in Christ that his love and care for us will overrule our need for acceptance and honor this side of heaven. We will be able to withstand evil reports, or relentless scrutiny, or unfair criticism because our souls will learn to find our rest in God alone (Psalm 62:1).

He will graciously enable us to embrace his call to us found in 1 Peter 3:9: "Do not repay evil for evil or reviling for reviling, but on the contrary, bless, for to this you were called, that you may obtain a blessing." And what is that blessing? When God's purposes are all fulfilled and all wrongs finally righted, God will bear a true witness about his servants. When friends or students or family or church members slander or even abandon you, you remain in good company—Jeremiah, Paul, and other heroic saints. Remember that God will have the last word about you—about your husband—and your kind King will bear a true witness about your godly heart and your true worth. We serve the God who remembers. "For God is not unjust so as to overlook your work and the love that you have shown for his name in serving the saints, as you still do" (Hebrews 6:10).

So by God's grace and through his power, let's be wives who strive to control our tongues and bear up under false accusations. "When reviled, we bless; when persecuted, we endure; when slandered, we entreat" (1 Corinthians 4:12–13). Jesus did. In fact, his brutal execution was based on false testimony (Matthew 26:57–62), yet even during his agony on the cross, he did not lash out. The Bible says that Jesus entrusted himself to him who judges rightly (1 Peter 2:23). We can too.

We find in Jesus a sympathetic high priest who was brutally tortured and murdered because men slandered him. At the cross

Jesus absorbed those lies—and every lie or rumor concerning you—and in turn he was gentle and meek and gave back love as he entrusted himself to his Father. And he says, "Follow me—take up your cross and entrust yourself to my Father. It's going to be all right. Your labor for him is never in vain" (see 1 Corinthians 15:58).

Day by Day

Serve Christ with wholehearted devotion and let him be the judge of how well you served. What does that look like day by day?

Try to *receive any persecution as from the Lord* to whom you have dedicated your whole life. It had to pass through his all-encircling protective Holy Spirit shield before it ever landed upon your experience. He is allowing it for some mighty purpose. Either he is capricious and cruel, *or* he has something good planned out in which he has asked you to take a part. We follow the one who brought only good to others, yet was brutally killed because other religious leaders were threatened by his ministry. Jesus Christ understands. He cares. Lean into his sword-scarred chest and let him wrap his nail-scarred hands around your sagging shoulders.

Continue to *cry out* to him. Even when he seems to be silent, continue to press in. Ray's dad used to tell me, "Jani, waiting is what faith does until God shows up." Be willing to wait. Keep looking to him.

Find a verse—a promise—to cling to. Camp on it, memorize it, meditate on it, and recite it to each other in the dark hours. A wise Christian counselor gave us this assignment when we were in a deep, dark pit because of slander. Our verse was 1 Peter 5:10, and God is indeed fulfilling it in our lives:

> After you have suffered a little while, the God of all grace, who has called you to his eternal glory in Christ, will himself restore, confirm, strengthen, and establish you. (1 Peter 5:10)

We couldn't see God fulfilling that promise in our lives for several years. But now, looking back, we are amazed at God's faithfulness. He can be trusted. Eventually every word of God will prove true. He cannot lie. Ask God for that verse meant for you in this painful situation. He is faithful. His timing may be different from yours, but he is faithful to fulfill every promise he has ever made.

Stop the comparison game. Do not fuss, talk about, worry, or fret over how other servants might seem to be thriving, succeeding, and flourishing. Keep your heart at home. Remember this:

> He who lives forever more
> > trod this earthly path before,
> Knows its dangers, knows its grief,
> > He will send your soul relief.[10]

—————————— A LETTER TO YOUR PASTOR ——————————

Dear Pastor,

Ray and I too understand how it feels to be ground to dust in the rumor mill. Like you, your wife may feel hurt, fearful, vulnerable, helpless. Ask her to share her heart with you. You could read and talk through Psalm 55 together: "It is not an enemy who taunts me—then I could bear it. . . . But it is you . . . my familiar friend. . . . My companion stretched out his hand against his friends; he violated his covenant" (vv. 12–13, 20).

Or you could turn to Psalm 109 and read together the first five verses. As the psalmist did, give yourselves to prayer. Let this hard time draw you closer together rather than drive a wedge between you. And then find a promise in Scripture that you can claim together for this dark time. Stand firm on that promise, looking to your promise-keeping God. Do not let the enemy win!

Grateful for his promises,

Jani

12

Help! Remind Me
Why We Do This

AFTER SHARING SOME of the overwhelming discouragements
of their past few years in ministry, the email from my younger
friend ended like this: "Sometimes I just need strong reminders of why we do what we do and why we shouldn't give up."
Strong reminders of *why*. Yes, we all need those. So in this final
chapter, let's remind ourselves why we do this.

Why Do We Do What We Do?

In the midst of demanding expectations, declining church
growth, and failing friendships, why do we do what we do?

It is one thing to be looked down on by the world around
you. But it is something else altogether to be humiliated and
even abandoned by the ones for whom you have poured out your
life—indeed, the very ones who asked you to come and serve
among them. Why do we do this? Why do we choose to absorb
the shame and sadness and carry on in ministry?

We make this choice—and it is a choice—because Christ has chosen us, and now we love him! We follow the one who was betrayed and abandoned by his closest friends. Some of that shame will spill over into our ministries as we follow in his footsteps. What are we to do? We long to be worthy of such a privilege but recoil from what this requires. What does it mean for me—not that other ministry wife who seems to have it so much easier, but for me—to take up my own cross and follow Christ? What does it look like to lose my life for his sake (Matthew 10:38–39)?

Elisabeth Elliot is one of my heroes. Please don't miss out on the depth of her faith as seen through her books. In *A Path through Suffering* she writes:

> Do the ways of God seem strange to some who are honestly seeking only to be good and faithful servants? There are strong winds, silent years of stress, deaths to be died. The One we serve has not left us without inside information as to the why. All who would bring souls to God must do so through surrender and sacrifice. This is what loving God means, a continual offering, a pure readiness to give oneself away, a happy obedience. There is no question, "But what about me?" for all the motivation is love. All interests, all impulses, all energies are subjugated to that supreme passion.[11]

That love springs from our faith. This kind of faith goes deep and waits long, even in the midst of pain. Our faith doesn't resolve our pain, it lives with it, enduring with patience through the power of his might (Colossians 1:11). Then in God's own way, he gets the glory and we get the joy.

Why Should We Keep Going?

I don't know the particular wave of hardship that might be breaking over you now, but I do know that God is allowing it and that he can be trusted. He sees this storm you're in, where headway is so painful because of all that is against you (Mark 6:45–52). He is using this very storm to help complete the great work which he began in you many years ago (Philippians 1:6). Hang on, and let this storm sweep you deeper into your Father's arms. It is only those who need him who draw close to his heart. Keep looking to him, keep crying out, keep trusting that his word is true for *you*—because it is!

Learn to embrace the God you serve in deeper, more personal ways. He sees. He understands. He is the God of restoration. "He restores my soul" (Psalm 23:3). Remember the big picture.

He chose you in Christ before time began, and created you to walk in specific good works:

> He chose us in him before the foundation of the world, that we should be holy and blameless before him. (Ephesians 1:4)

> For we are his workmanship, created in Christ Jesus for good works, which God prepared beforehand, that we should walk in them. (Ephesians 2:10)

He formed every day of your life, and recorded them in his book, before you ever took your first breath:

> Your eyes saw my unformed substance;
> in your book were written, every one of them,

the days that were formed for me,

when as yet there was none of them. (Psalm 139:16)

Everything you do for Jesus is of consequence, bearing weight in light of eternity:

Therefore, my beloved brothers, be steadfast, immovable, always abounding in the work of the Lord, knowing that in the Lord your labor is not in vain. (1 Corinthians 15:58)

You are a woman of sincerity, a fragrant, life-giving offering to the God who commissioned you. In his sight, you speak in Christ to others:

But thanks be to God, who in Christ always leads us in triumphal procession, and through us spreads the fragrance of the knowledge of him everywhere. For we are the aroma of Christ to God among those who are being saved and among those who are perishing, to one a fragrance from death to death, to the other a fragrance from life to life. Who is sufficient for these things? For we are not, like so many, peddlers of God's word, but as men of sincerity, as commissioned by God, in the sight of God we speak in Christ. (2 Corinthians 2:14–17)

Keep hanging on! Don't give up. Stand firm against the wiles of the devil, who seeks to destroy you and your man.

If you are weak, if you are sad, if you are discouraged, what of it? God gives himself *all the more* to those who need him. Your discouragement is not a problem to him. He doesn't scoff at your need. Your weakness is one of his strategies to draw you into ever deeper and more significant communion with him—the only one who can truly understand and satisfy your longings.

Here are four things I tell myself when I'm tempted to let discouragement reign in my heart.

1. *I volunteered to marry this pastor.* I wasn't forced into it! In fact, I even asked the Lord to cause Ray to fall in love with me! (I'm sure at least some of you can identify.) So what will I do with the Lord's answer of, "Yes, my daughter. I will give my servant to you as your husband, and I will give you to him as his helper. You are my favor to Ray Ortlund Jr. (Prov. 18:22)"? How will I continue to respond to God's answer to my prayer?

2. *Do not be surprised that ministry is hard.* This took me some time to accept. I'd thought life—and especially my life in ministry—would be easier than it has been. But even the hardest difficulties have become precious to me as I have been cared for by God. He sees (Genesis 16:13). He knows (John 10:14). He cares (1 Peter 5:7). And he rewards those who seek him (Hebrews 6:10). Life is hard—but God is still good. His goodness trumps the hardness at every point along the way. The harder my life is, the more I need him, and that is the most wonderful blessing in all of life—more of Jesus!

3. *Remember the cross.* Jesus gets my lonely days. He understands what slander feels like. He knows what it means to work hard. He experienced sufferings way beyond the trivial trials I experience. I am his servant. My whole life is an offering. Therefore I can hold it loosely, with an open-handed love. If I don't base my happiness on my hopes and dreams, I have less to lose when they aren't fulfilled according to my expectations. "He who did

not spare his own Son but gave him up for us all, how will he not also with him graciously give us all things?" (Romans 8:32).

4. *This is not the end of my story.* My earthly life had a beginning and it will have an end. My life in Christ also had a beginning, but it will *never* end. He revealed himself to me in irresistible love and adopted me as his daughter and has cared for me every day of my life. He has gone ahead of me and is preparing a place for me when my earthly life ends. How would he ever desert me on this bridge to that place? When darkness seems to cloud my heart and my path forward, I go to his word and find a promise to cling to as a lamp to my feet and a light to my path (Psalm 119:105).

———

Why should we keep going? Because Jesus is worth it! Psalm 84:11 is still true. The Lord God will be both your director and protector. He will give you favor and honor. Don't give up too soon! He will never hold back any good thing from his righteous ones. Now let him prove it to you and that pastor you're married to. May God bless you more and more in your ministry marriage. We will meet soon and serve our Lord together forever. I can't wait!

——— A LETTER TO YOUR PASTOR ———

Dear Pastor,

Your wife has read this book because she wants her ministry marriage to be healthy and satisfying. Why not ask her to share with you how God has been speaking to her here? After she shares her heart with you, let her know how you are doing. The two of you are in this ministry marriage together as intimate allies, by God's grace, for his glory and your joy. May he use you and your marriage in beautiful ways to further his kingdom!

God bless you,

Jani

Appendix

Scriptural Prayers for My Husband

LET'S BE WOMEN WHO PRAY for our pastor husbands. Prayer is for drawing down new blessings. What a privilege! "Continue steadfastly in prayer, being watchful in it with thanksgiving" (Colossians 4:2).

Who knows your husband better than you—what he wants, what he needs? Who loves him more? Pray long; pray hard. I like to call these kinds of prayers, prayers that PUSH: "Pray Until Something Happens," from Luke 18:1–7. Let's persist in prayer with holy determination, using Scripture as the foundation for our requests. Following are some Scriptures I pray over my pastor husband.

Prayer for His Soul

Dear Heavenly Father,

Thank you for giving my husband the gift of faith. Now please awaken in him an even deeper thirst for you, an urgent longing that can be satisfied only by spending time with you (Psalm 42:1–2). Please fill him with your power, not his own, through the Spirit of the Lord (Micah 3:8). Give him the motivation and perseverance he needs to devote himself to prayer and the ministry of the word (Acts 6:4; Ephesians 6:18). Make his Christian life one of miracle, not management.

Father, lead him to walk in a manner worthy of the Lord (Colossians 1:10), helping him to discern what would please you (Ephesians 5:10). Enable him to overflow with ever-increasing love and knowledge and all discernment (Philippians 1:9). Let him become distinguished in his generation as a man full of integrity because of his excellent spirit (Daniel 6:3–4).

Lord, grant him many years of vigorous good health to serve you. Give him wisdom with his body, your temple (1 Corinthians 6:18–19). Help him to discipline his body and keep it under control (1 Corinthians 9:27). Give him the strength to not set before his eyes anything that is worthless (Psalm 101:3), and help him to run from all sexual immorality (1 Corinthians 6:17).

Prayer for His Family

Dear Heavenly Father,

Thank you that he has given me the honor of being his wife. May he find our marital love ever more captivating and delightful (Proverbs 5:15–20). May he spend his life cheerfully fulfilling his marital vows, as he seeks to love me as Christ loved the church (Ephesians 5:25) and live with me in an understanding way (1 Peter 3:7).

May our children show the nurture and beauty of a strong Christian home (Psalm 144:12), with an authentic faith lived out in hope and obedience, a faith that they will be able to pass along to their children and grandchildren (Psalm 78:6–7). May these kids be mighty in the land and blessed by the Lord (Psalm 112:2). May my husband, by your grace, leave a legacy of Spirit-filled, stable, and steadfast followers of Jesus Christ to the tenth generation (Isaiah 44:3–5).

Prayer for His Ministry

O Lord,

Please enlarge my husband's influence and keep your hand on him (1 Chronicles 4:10) as he seeks to make the best use of his time and tries to understand what your will is for him (Ephesians 5:15–17). Bless him with fruit in every good work, and grant him an ever-increasing knowledge of you (Colossians 1:10).

Help him not to preach himself, but Jesus Christ as Lord (2 Corinthians 4:5), and give him the discernment to rightly handle the word of truth (2 Timothy 2:15). May his teaching and preaching be full of integrity, dignity, and sound speech so that his critics would have nothing evil to say about him (Titus 2:15).

May he gladly spend and be spent for others' eternal good (Corinthians 12:15). And please, dear Father, help him to fight the good fight, finishing the race that you have marked out for him, as he keeps the faith to his dying breath (2 Timothy 4:7).

How I love you, and how I love him.

In Jesus's holy name,

Amen

Notes

1. I am grateful for the beautiful example here of Sarah Edwards, wife of Jonathan Edwards. See Doreen Moore, *Good Christians, Good Husbands?* (Fearn, Scotland: Christian Focus, 2004), 94.
2. Richard A. Swenson, *Margin: Restoring Emotional, Physical, Financial, and Time Reserves to Overloaded Lives*, rev. ed. (Colorado Springs, CO: NavPress, 2004).
3. For further teaching on Sabbath rest, please see my book *His Loving Law, Our Lasting Legacy: Living the Ten Commandments and Giving Them to Our Children* (Wheaton, IL: Crossway, 2007), chap. 4.
4. John Gottman and Joan DeClaire, *The Relationship Cure: A Five-Step Guide to Strengthening Your Marriage, Family, and Friendships* (New York: Crown, 2001), 16–18.
5. Portions of this chapter were previously published in "I Haven't Seen Them for a While," Revive Our Hearts website, January 11, 2016, https://www.reviveourhearts.com/leaders/blog/i-havent-seen-them-while/.
6. Ed Wheat and Gaye Wheat, *Intended for Pleasure: Sex Technique and Sexual Fulfillment in Christian Marriage* (Grand Rapids, MI: Baker, 2010).
7. Ann Landers, "The Metal Box," *Chicago Tribune*, June 6, 1998. Used by permission of Esther P. Lederer Trust and Creators Syndicate, Inc.
8. Edith Schaeffer, *Lifelines: The Ten Commandments for Today* (Wheaton, IL: Crossway, 1982), 189.
9. George MacDonald, *Malcolm*, ed. Michael Phillips (Minneapolis: Bethany, 1982), 174–75.
10. Eliza E. Hewitt, "Where His Voice Is Guiding," 1896.
11. Elisabeth Elliot, *A Path through Suffering* (Ann Arbor, MI: Servant, 1990), 101.

General Index

Wheat, Gary (*Intended for Pleasure*), 83

wife: as gift of God, 22; as nag, 34; as teacher, 59–60; as director, 61

woman, beauty of, 36

women: calling of, 22

worship, 75

zoo patrol, 25–26

Scripture Index